BASEBALL'S BEST
SLUGGERS

By Jon Scher

A
*Sports Illustrated
For Kids*
Book

Baseball's Best Sluggers by Jon Scher

A Sports Illustrated For Kids book/January 1997

Cover and interior design by Miriam Dustin
Cover photographs by Ron Vesely (Mark McGwire), Tom DiPace (Ken Griffey, Jr.), and Doug Pensinger/Allsport USA (Frank Thomas)

For information, address: Sports Illustrated For Kids

Baseball's Best Sluggers is published by Sports Illustrated For Kids, division of Time Inc. Its trademark is registered in the U.S. Patent and Trademark Office and in other countries. Sports Illustrated For Kids, 1271 Avenue of the Americas, New York, NY 10020

PRINTED IN THE UNITED STATES OF AMERICA
10 9 8 7 6 5 4 3 2 1

ISBN 1-886749-24-8

Baseball's Best Sluggers
is a production of Sports Illustrated For Kids Books:
Cathrine Wolf, Editorial Director, Margaret Sieck, Senior Editor (Project Editor); Stephen Thomas, Associate Editor;
Sherie Holder, Assistant Editor

CONTENTS

Introduction..5

Chapter 1: **Ken Griffey, Junior**.............6

Chapter 2: **Frank Thomas**...................13

Chapter 3: **Barry Bonds**.......................20

Chapter 4: **Mike Piazza**.......................27

Chapter 5: **Mo Vaughn**..........................33

Chapter 6: **Mark McGwire**..................41

Chapter 7: **Albert Belle**.......................49

Chapter 8: **Cecil Fielder**.......................57

INTRODUCTION

THIS IS NO TIME TO BE A PITCHER.

Baseball has become a power game. More great hitters are flexing their muscles today than ever before. These guys are bashing baseballs out of ballparks at an amazing rate.

For example, in 1996, 17 sluggers hit 40 or more home runs. Mark McGwire of the Oakland Athletics was the leader, with 52. The 28 major league teams combined for a record 4,962 home runs, and the Baltimore Orioles cracked a major league *team* record 257 homers.

Why are so many people hitting so many baseballs so far? Pitching is weak. Hitters are strong. They lift weights, and they work all year to stay in shape. Also, new ballparks such as Baltimore's Camden Yards and Denver's Coors Field are smaller than most older stadiums.

The baseballs may also be "juiced." Some people believe the balls are harder. Harder baseballs fly farther when they are hit.

Or maybe baseball fans are just lucky! Here's your chance to meet eight of the hard-hitters who are helping rewrite baseball history. When one of these players is on deck, stay in your seat!

Power hitters can be fun to watch even when they strike out. But when they connect . . . *wow!*

Crack! It's a long drive, way back . . . deep . . . that ball is going, going . . . it's GONE!

6

KEN GRIFFEY, JUNIOR

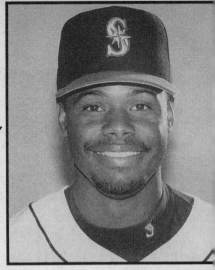

On August 24, 1995, Ken Griffey, Junior, saved baseball in Seattle.

The Seattle Mariners were trailing the New York Yankees, 7–6. There were two outs in the bottom of the ninth inning. It was a very important game for the Mariners. They had won 54 games and lost 55, and were in third place in the American League West.

The Mariners' playoff hopes were fading fast. So was their future. The team had been asking for a new stadium to replace its run-down home, the Kingdome. But fans in Seattle weren't excited about the team. Taxpayers were undecided: Should they spend millions of dollars to build a park for the Mariners or just let the team move away?

The game against the Yankees was the turning point. With back-to-back base hits, the Mariners tied the score, 7–7. Then Junior came to the plate. Yankee pitcher John Wetteland threw him a fastball. *Big* mistake.

Junior slashed his 31-ounce bat through the strike

zone. *Crack!* He raised his arms and pointed toward the roof. Junior knew the ball was gone. It landed in the right-field stands. Home run! The Mariners won, 9–7!

"That was the one that got us going," said Mariner manager Lou Piniella. "It wasn't just how we did it, but because *Junior* did it."

After that thrilling win, Seattle got *hot*. The Mariners won 25 of their last 36 regular-season games. For the first time, Mariner-mania struck Seattle. Fans packed the Kingdome. Millions more tuned in on TV and on the radio.

The Mariners came from 13 games behind to tie the California Angels for first place. Then they beat the Angels in a one-game playoff to win their first division title. The Mariners knocked off the Yankees, three games to two, in the A.L. division series. In the series, Junior hit five homers to tie a post-season record. He also scored the winning run in the final game.

After the season, the city decided to build the ballpark after all. It is scheduled to open in 1999. Instead of Century Park, maybe it ought to be called Griffey Stadium!

◆

Junior joined the Mariners in 1989. Since then, he has become one of the best — and most popular — players in all of baseball. Fans love to see his spectacular play in

COOL FACTS In the 1986 Connie Mack League World Series, for kids age 18 and under, 16-year-old Junior hit three homers in a game — one to leftfield, one to center, and one to right!

centerfield, his sweet swing, and his brilliant smile.

"People come out to root for him, to be swept up by his enthusiasm, and amazed by his talent," Manager Lou Piniella told *Sports Illustrated* in 1994.

Since 1989, Junior has batted over .300 six times. He has driven in more than 100 runs four times. He has won seven Gold Glove awards for fielding excellence. He has been selected for seven All-Star teams. He was named All-Star MVP in 1992. In 1994, he received a record 6.1 million All-Star votes from fans.

Junior resists being labeled a slugger. "I don't consider myself a home run hitter," he says. "But when I'm seeing the ball and hitting it hard, it will go out of the park."

Will it ever! Junior has bashed more than 40 homers in a season three times. In 1996, he hit 49. At this rate, he could hit more than 500 career homers!

"I never saw Babe Ruth hit, but we're possibly seeing another one in the making," says Lou Piniella. "I'll tell you this: He's the best I've ever been around."

◆

Junior grew up around major league baseball. His dad, Ken Griffey, Senior, was a star outfielder for the Cincinnati Reds in the 1970's *(see box on opposite page)*.

When Junior was 6 years old, he watched the Reds beat the Boston Red Sox in the 1975 World Series. In that era, the Cincinnati team was called "The Big Red Machine" because of its many powerful hitters.

Junior loved to go to work with his dad. Hours before a game, Ken senior sometimes pitched batting practice to Junior and his brother on the Riverfront Stadium field.

Junior was a fast learner. He started playing Little League baseball at age 8. By the time he was 11, he was so good that his dad could not strike him out. After his second year at Moeller High School, in Cincinnati, Ohio, 16-year-old Junior competed against 18-year-olds in a summer league. Major league scouts were starting to notice his talent.

Junior had all five of the "tools" that major leaguers need. He could hit, hit with power, throw, run, and field. In June 1987, the Mariners selected him with the first pick in the draft. His dad negotiated Junior's contract. It included a $160,000 signing bonus.

Junior dashed through the minor leagues, starring in Bellingham, Washington; San Bernardino, California; and Burlington, Vermont. In April 1989, less than two years after he had turned pro, Junior made it to the major leagues. He was 19 years old.

◆

Junior's first major league at-bat was against the Oakland Athletics. He hit a double. Later that night, Ken

A BASEBALL FAMILY

Junior's dad, Ken Griffey, Senior, played for four teams in 19 seasons — the Cincinnati Reds, New York Yankees, Atlanta Braves, and Seattle Mariners. Ken senior batted over .300 seven times. Also in the family are Junior's mom, Alberta (who is known as Birdie); his brother, Craig, who was born the year after Junior; and his sister, Lathesia, who came along two years after Craig.

senior watched the replay on TV. "I'll tell you the truth: I cried," he said. The Griffeys had become the first father and son to play in the majors at the same time!

Success came easily for Junior. He didn't practice as hard as other players. He didn't have to. He didn't study other teams' pitchers. He didn't even learn their names. He wore his hat backward during warmups and always seemed to be laughing and joking around. To Junior, the game was simple. "I see the ball, I hit the ball," he said in 1990.

That summer, the Mariners signed a special player: Junior's dad! On August 31, 1990, the Griffeys trotted onto the field at the Kingdome. They were teammates for the first time. It was a historic, and emotional, night. "I didn't know what to think," said Junior. "I wanted to cry. I just stood there and looked at him in leftfield."

In his first at-bat, Ken senior singled. Junior then got a single of his own! On September 14, Ken senior blasted a home run off Kirk McCaskill of the California Angels. "That's the way you do it, son," Ken senior said when he reached home plate. Then Junior hit a homer too!

BLAST FROM THE PAST

Reggie Jackson hit 563 home runs from 1967 to 1987. Reggie had a powerful swing and a magnetic personality. He once hit three consecutive homers in one World Series game! Reggie told *Sports Illustrated* that "[Junior] is a shot in the arm for baseball. . . . He is creating excitement and making headlines just by his presence. There hasn't been anyone like that since . . . Reggie Jackson."

OTHER PEOPLE SAY . . .
"Junior has that golden smile. He is like a kid on the sandlot.... He always seems to be having more fun than the rest of us." — Frank Thomas, Chicago White Sox

The Griffeys played together in 15 games that season. Ken senior was impressed by his son. "He can be as good as he wants to be," said Ken senior.

Junior wants to be very good.

His dad retired in 1991, but Junior continues to polish the Griffey legend. In 1993, Junior tied a major league record by hitting a home run in eight consecutive games. In 1994, he was leading the majors with 40 homers in 111 games when the players' strike ended the season. He had been on target to break Roger Maris's single-season record of 61 homers. Would Junior have done it? Nobody knows.

Only injuries have slowed him down. He broke his left wrist in 1995 and missed half the season. In 1996, his right wrist was broken by a pitch, and he was out for 20 games.

Wherever he goes, Junior is mobbed by fans who want his autograph. To get away from all the attention, Junior and his wife, Melissa, hang out at home with their kids. Junior also loves to go fishing and jet skiing.

In 1996, Junior starred in an ad campaign for a shoe company. The ads pretended that Junior was running for president of the United States. But why would he want to do that? Being Ken Griffey, Junior, is a lot more fun!

PERSONAL STATS

Name: George Kenneth Griffey, Junior
Nickname: Junior
Height: 6′ 3″   **Weight:** 200 lbs.
Bats: Left   **Throws:** Left
Birth Date: November 21, 1969
Birthplace: Donora, Pennsylvania
Current Homes: Orlando, Florida, and Issaquah, Washington
Family: Melissa (wife), Trey Kenneth (son, born January 19, 1994), Taryn (daughter, born October 21, 1995)

MAJOR LEAGUE STATS
SEATTLE MARINERS

YEAR	AVG.	G	AB	R	H	HR	RBI	SO	BB	SB
1989	.264	127	455	61	120	16	61	83	44	16
1990	.300	155	597	91	179	22	80	81	63	16
1991	.327	154	548	76	179	22	100	82	71	18
1992	.308	142	565	83	174	27	103	67	44	10
1993	.309	156	582	113	180	45	109	91	96	17
1994	.323	111	433	94	140	40	90	73	56	11
1995	.258	72	260	52	67	17	42	53	52	4
1996	.303	140	545	125	165	49	140	104	78	16
TOTAL	.302	1,057	3,985	695	1,204	238	725	634	504	108

AP/WIDE WORLD PHOTO

FRANK THOMAS

When he was a 12-year-old Little Leaguer, Frank Thomas once bashed a home run into the top of a very tall pine tree. In high school, he blasted homers off buildings way beyond the outfield. In college, he hit one over a 45-foot-tall scoreboard.

When Frank joined the Chicago White Sox, fans and teammates couldn't believe how far his home runs traveled.

Ken "Hawk" Harrelson, a White Sox TV broadcaster, noted how Frank's homers often injured the confidence of the pitchers he faced. Hawk started calling Frank "The Big Hurt."

The nickname stuck. A legend was born!

◆

Frank is 6' 5" tall, and he weighs 257 pounds. He looks as if he could play pro football. But instead of pounding linebackers, he pounds pitchers. They *hate* to see him coming up to the plate.

"I wish they'd let us put on the catcher's mask and

shin guards," pitcher Dennis Martinez of the Cleveland Indians says of facing Frank. "Pitchers shouldn't be left out there alone with him."

For six seasons in a row, starting in 1991, Frank:

- ◆ batted over .300
- ◆ hit more than 20 homers
- ◆ drove in more than 100 runs
- ◆ scored more than 100 runs
- ◆ drew more than 100 walks.

No other major league player has ever done so much, so well, for so long.

Frank was the American League's Most Valuable Player in 1993 and 1994. Only 10 other players have won back-to-back MVP awards. He has hit 40 or more homers three times. Frank's lifetime batting average is .327!

Frank says, "I want to be one of those guys who make people say, 'Some of the things he did I don't think can ever be done again.' "

Frank wasn't always big. When he was born, in Columbus, Georgia, on May 27, 1968, he weighed

BLAST FROM THE PAST

Ted Williams starred for the Boston Red Sox between 1939 and 1960. Like Frank, he hit for a high average (.344), smacked plenty of home runs (521), and was very patient at the plate. Ted *refused* to swing at bad pitches. He walked more than 100 times in 11 different seasons!

seven pounds. That's an average weight for a baby.

The Thomas house was quite crowded. Frank was the fifth of six children. He has an older brother, Mike, and three older sisters, Gloria, Mary, and Sharon. Another sister, Pamela, was born in 1975, seven years after Frank.

Frank's parents worked hard to take care of their kids. His mom, Charlie Mae, was an inspector in a textile mill. His dad, Frank, Senior, worked at the local jail and was a deacon at a Baptist church.

While Frank's folks were at work, his older brother and sisters were responsible for him. When he wasn't in school, he spent most of his time playing sports at the Boys Club.

"I had to walk three or four miles down the railroad track to get there every day," Frank says.

◆

Disaster struck the Thomas family in 1977. In September, Frank's 2-year-old sister, Pamela, suddenly became very sick. She had to go to a hospital. Doctors found she had a life-threatening blood disease called leukemia.

Nine-year-old Frank was crushed by Pamela's illness. As the "babies" of the family, the two had grown very close.

Pamela remained in the hospital for weeks. She was treated with powerful drugs, which made her hair fall out. But when she came home, Pamela gave Frank a big smile.

Still, Pamela never got better. She died on Thanksgiving Day, 1977. "I was sad for a long time," Frank says. "Pamela was my favorite person, but I learned to move on. Life moves on."

On the day Pamela died, Frank dedicated himself to becoming a great athlete. He wanted to do it in honor of his sister. Later, he also decided to do whatever he could to help cure leukemia.

Frank has followed through. Since joining the White Sox, Frank has raised hundreds of thousands of dollars for leukemia research. Every time Frank signs an autograph for a fan, he asks for one dollar. Then he matches it with a dollar of his own. The money goes into The Frankie Fund to help fight the disease.

Today, doctors can do much more to help kids like Pamela. Some are even cured!

After he lost his sister, Frank stayed busy by playing sports. He already towered over the other kids. At age 9, he was 5' 6" tall. He played football in a league with 12-year-olds.

Frank grew to 6' 4" by the time he became a sophomore at Columbus High School. He starred in football, basketball, and baseball. Frank's dedication to sports was starting to pay off.

COOL FACTS Frank has an amazing memory. Once, in Cleveland, he was signing an autograph for a young man. He glanced at the man's face. "That's the last time I sign for you for a while," Frank told the man. "I've signed for you three times in the past two years. Am I right?" He was right!

OTHER PEOPLE SAY . . .
"Frank is too big to be a man and too small
to be a horse." — former White Sox teammate
Steve "Psycho" Lyons

In football, he caught plenty of passes as a tight end, and he kicked extra points. His senior year, he made 15 points in 15 tries — a perfect record! In basketball, he led the team in scoring and rebounding. In baseball, he was the team's slugging, strong-armed centerfielder.

The next spring, Frank decided that baseball would be his ticket to fame and fortune. He batted .329 and belted eight home runs. But then, during his senior year, he was recruited by the football coaches at Auburn (Alabama) University. Frank figured he could fall back on football if he wasn't drafted into the major leagues. He accepted Auburn's offer of a football scholarship.

That gave pro baseball scouts the wrong idea. They thought he wanted to play football more than baseball. In June 1986, Frank wasn't drafted by a single major league baseball team. He was so upset that he went to his room and cried. Then he grew angry. "The scouts goofed," he says.

At Auburn, Frank played tight end for one season. He was hit from behind and hurt his knee. After that, he concentrated on baseball.

Frank played first base and set a school record with 49 career homers. Still, in 1988, he was left off the U.S. Olympic Baseball Team. Finally, in 1989 the White Sox selected him with the seventh pick in the draft.

Frank needed only 180 minor league games to prepare for the majors. The White Sox called him up in
August 1990. He has been scaring major league pitchers
to death ever since.

◆

The White Sox haven't made the playoffs since
1993. That year they lost, four games to two, to the
Toronto Blue Jays in the American League Championship
Series. The Jays were so afraid of Frank's bat that they
intentionally walked him in the third inning of Game 6 —
with the bases loaded! Although that forced in one run,
Toronto got out of the jam and won the game, 6–3.

Frank misses the excitement and pressure of playoff
baseball. "I love big games, big series. I relish the opportunity to rise to the top," Frank says. "I want to be the guy
there with two out and the bases loaded trying to get a hit."

Frank has been criticized by fans and other players
for being too picky about pitches. While most power hitters swing at anything close to the strike zone, Frank
waits for a good pitch to hit. He believes in getting on
base. To Frank, runs batted in (RBIs) are more important
than homers. A bases-clearing double gives him more
satisfaction than a bases-empty home run.

Sometimes, he *knows* he's going to get a hit. "There's
definitely times," Frank says, "when I can see the ball out
of the pitcher's hand and I know whether it's going to be
inside or outside, curveball or change-up. I can tell it. In
those high times, I just smack that thing as hard as I can.
I'm going to try to hurt you."

Big!

PERSONAL STATS

Name: Frank Edward Thomas, Junior
Nickname: The Big Hurt
Height: 6' 5"   **Weight:** 257 lbs.
Bats: Right   **Throws:** Right
Birth Date: May 27, 1968
Birthplace: Columbus, Georgia
Current Home: Burr Ridge, Illinois
Family: Elise (wife), Sterling (son, born July 14, 1992), Sloan (daughter, born March 23, 1994)

MAJOR LEAGUE STATS
CHICAGO WHITE SOX

YEAR	AVG.	G	AB	R	H	HR	RBI	SO	BB	SB
1990	.330	60	191	39	63	7	31	54	44	0
1991	.318	158	559	104	178	32	109	112	138	1
1992	.323	160	573	108	185	24	115	88	122	6
1993	.317	153	549	106	174	41	128	54	112	4
1994	.353	113	399	106	141	38	101	61	109	2
1995	.308	145	493	102	152	40	111	74	136	3
1996	.349	141	527	110	184	40	134	70	109	1
TOTAL	.327	930	3,291	675	1,077	222	729	513	770	17

BARRY BONDS

Barry Bonds was born to play baseball. His father, Bobby Bonds, was a three-time All-Star. Bobby combined power and speed in his 14-year major league career. He hit 332 homers and stole 461 bases from 1968 to 1981.

Barry's distant cousin, Hall of Famer Reggie Jackson, hit 563 homers in 21 seasons. And Barry's godfather, Willie Mays, whacked 660 homers in 22 years. Willie is in the Hall of Fame, too. Many people think he was the greatest all-around player in baseball history!

Barry, the leftfielder for the San Francisco Giants, is a great all-around player, too. He has hit 30 or more homers and stolen 30 or more bases in the same season four times. Only his father, Bobby, did it more often. (Bobby was in the 30-30 club five times.)

In 1996, Barry did something his dad, his cousin, and his godfather *never* did: He hit 42 homers and stole 40 bases. Barry became the second man in history to join the 40-40 club. (In 1988, Jose Canseco hit 42 homers and stole 40 bases for the Oakland A's.)

Barry is one of only eight players to win three Most Valuable Player awards. He is the only man to be voted MVP three times in four seasons (1990, 1991, and 1993). No one in baseball history has ever won *four* MVPs. Before he retires, Barry could become the first.

Barry is awesome in the outfield, too. Since 1990, he has won six Gold Glove awards for fielding excellence.

As former New York Mets manager Jeff Torborg once said, "Barry belongs in a higher league."

◆

Barry was born on July 24, 1964, while his dad was playing in the Giants' minor league system. By the time Barry was 6, Bobby had developed into an All-Star.

Bobby played leftfield for the Giants. The center-fielder was Willie Mays, Barry's godfather. During batting practice in San Francisco's Candlestick Park, Barry loved to shag fly balls with his father and godfather. Barry competed with them for fly balls. Sometimes Barry would win!

◆

Barry grew up in San Carlos, California, a suburb of San Francisco. He was a star in the San Carlos Little

COOL FACTS Barry is a member of the Screen Actors Guild. He played himself in two movies, *Jane's House* and *Rookie of the Year*. He also appeared in episodes of two TV shows, *In Living Color* and *Beverly Hills 90210*.

League. Bobby sat in his car while he watched his son play, to avoid attracting attention to himself.

Barry played baseball, basketball, and football at Serra High, an all-boys private school in the nearby town of San Mateo. "He loved the limelight," his basketball coach, Kevin Donahue, told *Sports Illustrated* in 1993. "He loved to take over the game with two minutes to go."

When Barry was a senior, he batted .467 and was regarded as one of the country's best high school baseball players. After he graduated from high school in 1982, the Giants made him a second-round draft pick. They offered him a $70,000 signing bonus. His father wanted the Giants to pay Barry $75,000, but the team said no. So, instead, Barry accepted a scholarship to Arizona State University.

◆

At Arizona State, Barry blossomed into an All-America outfielder. As a junior, in 1985, his 23 homers in

BLAST FROM THE PAST

Barry's father, Bobby Bonds, blazed a trail for his son to follow. Bobby was only the fourth man in history to hit 30 homers and steal 30 bases in the same season. Bobby did it a record five times! Through the 1996 season, Bobby (332) and Barry (334) had combined for 666 major league home runs — more than any other father and son. "You know what I'm proudest of?" Bobby says. "That now I'm known as Barry Bonds' father."

62 games led the team. He batted .347 during his three-year college career.

Barry's personality, however, annoyed many of his teammates. He didn't have many friends.

"I liked Barry Bonds," his Arizona State coach, Jim Brock, once said. "But I never saw a teammate care about him. Part of it would be his being rude, inconsiderate, and self-centered. He bragged about the money he turned down, and he popped off about his dad. I don't think he ever figured out what to do to get people to like him."

The Pittsburgh Pirates liked him. They chose Barry with the sixth pick in the 1985 draft. He spent the 1985 season with the Class A Prince William Pirates, and then jumped all the way to the Triple-A Hawaii Islanders.

In late May 1986, Pirate general manager Syd Thrift watched Barry play for the Islanders. During batting practice, Barry walloped six balls over the rightfield fence.

"Any good hitter can do that," Mr. Thrift told Barry, who is lefthanded. "I'd like to see you hit a few over the leftfield fence."

"Fine," Barry said. Then he whacked five balls over the fence in left!

"Is that good enough for you?" Barry asked.

"Fine," Mr. Thrift replied. When Mr. Thrift flew back to Pittsburgh, he took Barry with him. After only 115 minor league games, Barry was moving up. The up-and-coming Pirates had a star they could build a team around.

◆

Barry became the Pirates' centerfielder and leadoff hitter. As he got better and better, so did the team. In

1990, Barry batted .301 with 33 homers and a league-high 52 stolen bases in 151 games. Pittsburgh won the National League Eastern Division title that year.

The Pirates won three straight NL Eastern Division titles, but they lost in the playoffs each time. Barry was part of the problem. His hot bat turned cold in the post-season. In 18 playoff games for the Pirates over those three years, he batted .191 with only one home run.

After the 1992 season, the cash-poor Pirates decided they couldn't afford to keep Barry. He accepted an offer from his father's old team, the Giants. Barry signed a six-year, $43.75 million contract. He became the highest paid player in baseball at the time. Bobby was the Giants' batting coach. Now he and Barry could work side-by-side!

San Francisco's investment paid off right away. Barry batted .336 in 1993, with 46 homers and 29 steals. He won his third MVP award. He helped the Giants win 103 games, although they just missed making the playoffs.

In the strike-shortened 1994 season, Barry hit 37 homers in only 112 games. And in 1995, he had his third 30-30 season, with 33 home runs and 31 stolen bases.

◆

Despite all his success — the three MVPs, the six Gold Gloves — Barry is not one of baseball's best-loved

OTHER PEOPLE SAY . . .

"Barry doesn't care what people think. All he's ever wanted is to be judged by what he's done on the field."
— former Pirate teammate Andy Van Slyke

COOL FACTS Barry's aunt, Rosie Bonds, was a track star. Rosie once held the U.S. women's record in the 80-meter hurdles. She was a member of the 1964 U.S. Olympic team!

superstars. During the 1990 playoffs, for example, Barry made fun of teammate Jeff King for getting injured. Pirate outfielder R.J. Reynolds told Barry to grow up. In response, Barry shoved a slice of pizza in R.J.'s face!

In response to his critics, Barry points to his stats and his impressive work habits. During the off-season he works out five hours a day, five days a week.

"Since I was a kid, I've had a stamp on my neck," Barry says. "People say Barry Bonds has a bad attitude and only thinks of himself. Who else am I supposed to think about out there?"

But Barry is working to change his image. He was honored in late 1996 for giving more than $100,000 to the Adopt a Special Kid program in the San Francisco Bay Area. The program places kids with special needs in caring homes.

At the 1996 All-Star Game in Philadelphia, Barry was one of the most talkative players in the National League clubhouse. He gave interview after interview.

Barry says he expects to become the first man to win four MVP awards. He expects it to happen soon.

"I've never let down in my confidence," Barry says. "Because if you don't believe in yourself, no one else will."

PERSONAL STATS

Name: Barry Lamar Bonds
Height: 6′ 1″   **Weight:** 190 lbs.
Bats: Left   **Throws:** Left
Birth Date: July 24, 1964
Birthplace: Riverside, California
Homes: Murietta and Atherton, California
Family: Nikolai (son, born December 18, 1989), Shikari (daughter, born March 20, 1991)

MAJOR LEAGUE STATS
PITTSBURGH PIRATES

YEAR	AVG.	G	AB	R	H	HR	RBI	SO	BB	SB
1986	.223	113	413	72	92	16	48	102	65	36
1987	.261	150	551	99	144	25	59	88	54	37
1988	.283	144	538	97	152	24	58	82	72	17
1989	.248	159	580	96	144	19	58	93	93	32
1990	.301	151	519	104	156	33	114	83	93	52
1991	.292	153	510	95	149	25	116	73	107	43
1992	.311	140	473	109	147	34	103	69	127	39

SAN FRANCISCO GIANTS

YEAR	AVG.	G	AB	R	H	HR	RBI	SO	BB	SB
1993	.336	159	539	129	181	46	123	79	126	29
1994	.312	112	391	89	122	37	81	43	74	29
1995	.294	144	506	109	149	33	104	83	120	31
1996	.308	158	517	122	159	42	129	76	151	40
TOTAL	.288	1,583	5,537	1,121	1,595	334	993	871	1,082	380

MiKE PiAZZA

Mike Piazza couldn't believe his good fortune. It was July 9, 1996. The Los Angeles Dodger catcher was standing near home plate at jam-packed Veterans Stadium, in Philadelphia, Pennsylvania.

Mike grew up in Phoenixville, a town outside Philadelphia. For years, Mike and his dad, Vince, often came and cheered for the Philadelphia Phillies.

Now Mike was back, as the starting catcher for the National League in the Major League Baseball All-Star Game. He was about to catch the ceremonial first pitch from Hall of Fame third baseman Mike Schmidt, the greatest player in Phillie history.

"That's when it all hit me," Mike said after the game. "I'm catching Mike Schmidt, my idol. My family's in the stands in my hometown. Playing here is always a thrill, but it was especially thrilling tonight."

Mike rose to the occasion. By hitting a homer and a

run-scoring double, he helped the National League beat the American League, 6–0. Mike was named the All-Star MVP!

As Mike held the trophy, he thought back to what his dad had often said as they watched the Phillies play. "If you work hard," Mr. Piazza told Mike, "dreams do come true."

◆

Mike was born on September 4, 1968. His dad owned a struggling used-car business. His mom, Veronica, stayed home to take care of Mike and his four brothers.

In 1976, when Mike was 7, Mr. Piazza took him to Veterans Stadium for the first time. They watched Mike Schmidt hit two home runs. From then on, Mike Piazza knew he wanted to become a professional baseball player.

Mr. Piazza encouraged Mike. He built a backyard batting cage and bought a pitching machine. After work, Mr. Piazza often rushed home to pitch batting practice.

"I was out there every day," Mike says. "I would come home from school, get a snack, watch cartoons, and then hit. Every spring I would see that I was hitting the ball farther and farther."

At night, Mike went down to the basement to hit some more. He leaned a mattress against a wall, and smacked balls off a tee into the mattress.

Although Mike hit .442 with 11 home runs as a

COOL FACTS Mike loves to play the drums. "I'm an aggressive person, and I needed an outlet to vent my frustrations," he says. "You know, to hit something."

OTHER PEOPLE SAY . . .

"Mike hits it harder than I did when I was 16. I guarantee you, this kid will hit the ball. I never saw anyone who looked better at his age."
— Hall of Fame slugger Ted Williams, after seeing Mike hit at age 15

senior at Phoenixville High, he was a slow runner. Major league baseball scouts were not impressed. He was passed over in the 1986 draft.

◆

Mike enrolled at the University of Miami, Florida. He played one season at Miami, but he wasn't able to crack the starting lineup. Mike transferred to Miami Dade North Community College. There, he batted .364.

Tommy Lasorda, then the Los Angeles Dodger manager, had been a childhood friend (and was a distant cousin) of Mr. Piazza. Mr. Lasorda is the godfather of Mike's youngest brother, Tommy. When the Dodgers played in Philadelphia, Mr. Lasorda often invited the Piazza kids to be Dodger batboys.

Mr. Lasorda begged the Dodgers to do him a favor and draft Mike in 1988. They did — in the 62nd round. Mike was the 1,390th player selected!

The Dodgers had better prospects ahead of him at first base. Mike went to Dodger Stadium for a tryout, and clobbered balls into the upper deck. Still, scouting director Ben Wade wasn't sure about signing him.

"If he was a *catcher* who could hit balls into the

seats like that, would you sign him?" Mr. Lasorda asked Mr. Wade.

"Sure," Mr. Wade replied. "But he's a first baseman."

"He's a catcher now," Mr. Lasorda growled.

Mike agreed to become a catcher. The Dodgers signed him to a minor league contract. In 1989, they sent him to Salem, Oregon, to play in a rookie league.

◆

Mike became known as one of the hardest workers in the entire Dodger organization. After the 1989 season, Mike asked the Dodgers to send him to their camp in the Dominican Republic. There he grew tougher and stronger.

By 1991, his third season in the minors, Mike was improving rapidly. He hit 29 homers for Class A Bakersfield, California. By the end of the 1992 season, Mike had made the major leagues!

In 1993, Mike hit 35 homers and was named National League Rookie of the Year. Mr. Lasorda was thrilled.

"Mike will be a marquee player for us, an impact

BLAST FROM THE PAST

Many people believe Mike is the best-hitting catcher since Johnny Bench. Johnny played for the Cincinnati Reds from 1967 to 1983. He had a powerful swing and a rocket launcher for a right arm. In 1970, Johnny hit 45 homers and drove in 148 runs. In 1,742 games behind the plate, Johnny hit 327 homers — a National League record for catchers.

COOL FACTS Mike, who lives near Hollywood, has been able to get small parts in some television shows and in the movie *Spy Hard*. Mike tried out for a role as a catcher in a baseball movie called *The Fan*, but didn't get it. "I'm not convincing enough to play a catcher? Come on," Mike complained.

player," he told *Sports Illustrated*. "I asked the Dodgers to draft him as a favor. And, thank God, they did."

Mike had no trouble learning to hit in the major leagues. Over his first three seasons, he crushed an impressive 91 homers. Catching was harder to learn. At first, he was unsure of himself. Pitchers complained that he was afraid to voice his opinion about what pitches they should throw.

Gradually, Mike won the pitchers' respect. Now he is one of the best catchers in the majors. He has been compared with great-hitting catchers of the past, such as Hall of Famers Johnny Bench *(see box on page 30)* and Roy Campanella.

Mike feels he's not ready for that type of comparison.

"Bench and Campanella?" Mike says. "I don't see myself in that class at all. They did it their whole career. Maybe five, seven years down the line, if I'm still doing what I'm doing, okay. But I've only played a few years, never won a World Series. I have much more to accomplish."

PERSONAL STATS

Name: Michael Joseph Piazza
Birth Date: September 4, 1968
Birthplace: Norristown, Pennsylvania
Current Home: Manhattan Beach, California
Height: 6' 3"   **Weight:** 215 lbs.
Bats: Right   **Throws:** Right
Family: Vince (father); Veronica (mother);
Vince, Junior; Danny; Tony; Tommy (brothers)

MAJOR LEAGUE STATS
LOS ANGELES DODGERS

YEAR	AVG.	G	AB	R	H	HR	RBI	SO	BB	SB
1992	.232	21	69	5	16	1	7	12	4	0
1993	.318	149	547	81	174	35	112	86	46	3
1994	.319	107	405	64	129	24	92	65	33	1
1995	.346	112	434	82	150	32	93	80	39	1
1996	.336	148	547	87	184	36	105	93	81	0
TOTAL	.326	537	2,002	319	653	128	409	336	203	5

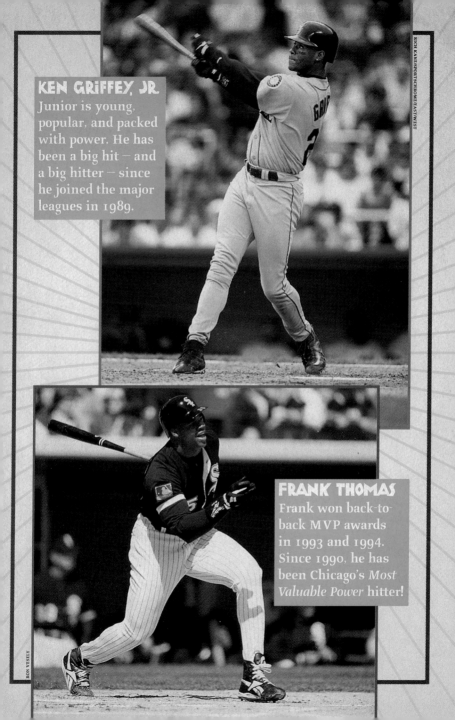

KEN GRIFFEY, JR.

Junior is young, popular, and packed with power. He has been a big hit – and a big hitter – since he joined the major leagues in 1989.

FRANK THOMAS

Frank won back-to-back MVP awards in 1993 and 1994. Since 1990, he has been Chicago's *Most Valuable Power* hitter!

V. J. LOVERO/SPORTS ILLUSTRATED

BARRY BONDS

Barry combines power and speed. He can get around the bases by hitting homers or by stealing! He has won the National League MVP award three times.

MIKE PIAZZA

Multi-talented Mike works well *behind* the plate as the National League's best catcher and *next* to the plate as a major slugger.

RON VESELY

MO VAUGHN

Mo has been scaring pitchers since his days in Little League. He may look mean, but he is really kind. He does a lot to help others, particularly kids.

MARK McGWIRE

This big man has had many injuries during his career. But they haven't held him back. In 1996, he hit 52 home runs!

ALBERT BELLE

A talented but troubled player, Albert is being paid $11 million a year to swing his sweet bat for the White Sox.

CECIL FIELDER

Cecil brought his size and power to the New York Yankees in 1996. He helped them win the World Series, for the first time since 1978!

MO VAUGHN

Mo Vaughn first learned to hit a baseball in the backyard of his home, in Norwalk, Connecticut. His mother taught him!

Shirley Vaughn liked to play softball. One day, when Mo was 2 or 3 years old, she took him outside and handed him a bat. The boy was right-handed, but Shirley was a lefty. He copied her left-handed swing. To this day, hitting is the only thing he does left-handed.

"She would throw this tennis ball to me, and I'd hit it," Mo says. "I remember I'd hit it over to other people's yards. I hit that ball *far!*"

Mrs. Vaughn must have been a good teacher. Mo grew up to become one of major league baseball's greatest hitters. In 1995, he batted .300 for the Boston Red Sox, with 39 homers and 126 runs batted in. He was named the American League's Most Valuable Player! In 1996, Mo had an even better year. He batted .326 with 44 homers and 143 RBIs.

That must make Shirley and her husband, Leroy, very proud of their son. They should be proud of him for another reason: He's one of the nicest people in sports. Mo has won many awards for his charity work. He loves helping kids. In 1994, he started the Mo Vaughn Youth Development Program for disadvantaged kids, in Dorchester, a suburb of Boston.

"I give $100,000 to the Boys and Girls Club every year," Mo told a reporter for *The Boston Globe* newspaper. "So what? Ballplayers make a lot of loot. I can't take it all with me, can I? If it's for a good cause, I don't mind giving the money. But I'll tell you what: When I give the money, the kids are gonna have to work hard and take care of their education."

Mo doesn't just donate money. He also donates his time. He gets to know kids on the streets, in schools, at Boys and Girls Clubs, and at his center.

One time, a group of 15-year-olds he was working with at his center started rudely talking back to him.

"These kids, man. Talking trash," Mo says. "I told

BLAST FROM THE PAST

Before Mo Vaughn, the last Red Sox slugger to win an MVP award was Jim Rice. In 1978, Jim batted .315 and led the American League in homers (46), RBIs (139), triples (15), and hits (213). He hit 382 homers during his 16-year career, and led the A.L. three times. Jim also helped the Red Sox reach the World Series in 1975 and 1986.

them, 'You all better straighten up. I'll spank you.' I'm serious. Some of these kids are out there disrespecting their elders. I won't have that."

Can you imagine being spanked by a 6' 1", 250-pound slugger? Faced with that, even the likes of Beavis and Butt-Head would behave!

◆

Mo got a head start on life. He was born on December 15, 1967, *nine weeks* before his mother was due to give birth. He weighed just three pounds, nine ounces. But he quickly grew to be bigger than most kids his age. His friends remember him as a roly-poly kid who was always smiling.

Mo's mom was an elementary school teacher, and his dad was a high school teacher and coach who had played in the National Football League for a year. Mo never liked school as much as his parents wanted him to. But he loved sports. "I played basketball. I played football. I ice-skated and played hockey," Mo says. "But baseball was it for me. I worked at baseball. I just liked to hit a baseball."

When Mo was 9 years old, he played in an organized baseball league for the first time. It was called "cap league" because the kids all got their own cap and T-shirt. Mo was his team's power-hitting third baseman. In several youth leagues, Mo played shortstop and pitcher, too. He once pitched a no-hitter!

◆

In Little League, when he was 12 years old, Mo remembers *crushing* the ball. "I hit something like 30 home runs in a 13-game season," he says.

People in Norwalk love to tell stories about young Mo's big home runs. They say he hit one over some trees. He hit another one over a house. Another one flew over the fence and bounced off a school building. Pitchers were so scared to face Mo, they often walked him intentionally — even with the bases loaded!

"When he was twelve, the first basemen used to move into rightfield when he came up," says former teammate Ed Luczkowski. "The rightfielders played up against the wall."

By the time he was a teenager, Mo was dreaming of a major league career. He was also working to make the dream come true. Mr. Vaughn drilled a hole through a baseball and hung it with a piece of twine on the back porch. Mo hit that ball 500 times a night. *Every* night.

◘

Mo's mom and dad taught him the value of hard work and the importance of charity. Each Christmas morning, Mo and his older sisters, Catherine and Donna, went with their parents to deliver food and presents to the homeless. "I was always taught that if I had the ability to help others, I should," Mo says.

To earn spending money, Mo had a lot of different jobs. He mopped floors at a supermarket, worked on a

OTHER PEOPLE SAY . . .
"What has Mo meant to this team? One word: Everything." — Red Sox shortstop John Valentin

COOL FACTS Mo is superstitious. He always dresses left to right. He puts on his left sock first, and then his right sock. He puts on his pants left-leg first. He puts on his shirt left-arm first. Mo says it's his lucky routine!

garbage truck, and helped pave roads and dig ditches.

Because his parents felt Mo wasn't taking school seriously enough in Norwalk, they sent him away to boarding school when he was in the ninth grade. He went to the Trinity-Pawling School, in Pawling, New York.

Trinity-Pawling was tough for Mo at first. As an African-American, he was in the minority. That had not been the case in school in Norwalk. Also, many of the kids were from wealthy families. "I had some adjustment problems," Mo says. "Now that I look back, it was an important experience for me. I learned to deal with problems head-on, through respect and communication."

Until Mo went to Trinity-Pawling, he was called by his given name: Maurice. "I got my nickname from the athletic director when I was in ninth grade," he says. "When he was calling me on the field, he couldn't yell Maurice fast enough, so he cut it down to Mo."

Mo became a star athlete at Trinity-Pawling. By the time he was a senior, he was popular with the other students, too. They elected him prefect, which is a leadership position in the student government.

The Philadelphia Phillies wanted to sign Mo to a

contract after he graduated from Trinity-Pawling, in 1986. Mo wanted to sign. But his parents said no. They insisted he accept a baseball scholarship to Seton Hall University, in New Jersey.

At the time, Mo was mad. Now he's glad.

"My parents made the right decision," Mo says. "I got a lot better baseball training in college, and I was able to be away from home, but not too far."

◆

Mo had a monster freshman year in college. He hit 28 homers in 53 games. Before that, the Seton Hall *career* home run record had been 27!

In three years at Seton Hall, Mo blasted 57 homers. He smacked one ball over the lights at a former minor league stadium in Connecticut. "But that wasn't my longest," he says. "I remember when we were playing Georgetown University down in Washington. It went 550 feet."

After his junior season, in 1989, the Red Sox drafted Mo in the first round. He skipped three levels of the minor league system and went directly to Double-A New Britain, Connecticut. In 1990, Mo batted .295, with 22 homers, at Triple-A Pawtucket, Rhode Island. Then, in the mid-

COOL FACTS Mo wears number 42 in honor of his hero, Hall of Famer Jackie Robinson. In 1947, Jackie became the first African American to play major league baseball. Jackie, a second baseman, wore number 42 for the Brooklyn Dodgers.

dle of the 1991 season, he was promoted to the Red Sox.

Mo figured he was a major leaguer for good. But when he got off to a slow start in 1992, the Red Sox sent him back to Pawtucket. Mo was steamed! "Since then, I've had a point to prove," he says. "I still do. It still burns inside me."

After 39 games in the minors, Mo returned to Boston. He became a much more patient hitter. He was more willing to wait for the right pitch. As a result, in 1993 he batted .297 with 29 homers. During the strike-shortened 1994 season, he hit .310 with 26 homers in only 111 games.

◆

Up close, Mo Vaughn is a scary-looking guy. He's big, his head is shaved, and his arms bulge with powerful muscles. He often has a mean look on his face.

But his friends, fans, and family aren't fooled. They know he's a nice guy. "Maurice still gives us all hugs, me, my husband, and the girls, whenever we get together," Mrs. Vaughn told Jack Cavanaugh of *The New York Times* newspaper. "He really hasn't changed much over the years. He doesn't burst out laughing on the field anymore, but we know he's still having fun."

And he's still listening to his Mom's batting tips. Once, when Mo was in a slump, his mom noticed something while watching him on TV. "You have to move closer to the plate," Mrs. Vaughn said. "You're too far away."

Mo took the advice. "My mom was right," he says. "Soon as I moved closer, I began to hit again."

Mother *still* knows best!

PERSONAL STATS

Name: Maurice Samuel Vaughn
Nicknames: Mo, Hit Dog
Height: 6' 1"   **Weight:** 240 lbs.
Bats: Left   **Throws:** Right
Birth Date: December 15, 1967
Birthplace: Norwalk, Connecticut
Current Home: Easton, Massachusetts
Family: Shirley (mother); Leroy (father);
Catherine and Donna (sisters)

MAJOR LEAGUE STATS
BOSTON RED SOX

YEAR	AVG.	G	AB	R	H	HR	RBI	SO	BB	SB
1991	.260	74	219	21	57	4	32	43	26	2
1992	.234	113	355	42	83	13	57	67	47	3
1993	.297	152	539	86	160	29	101	130	79	4
1994	.310	111	394	65	122	26	82	112	57	4
1995	.300	140	550	98	165	39	126	150	68	11
1996	.326	161	635	118	207	44	143	154	95	2
TOTAL	.295	751	2,692	430	794	155	541	656	372	26

MARK McGWIRE

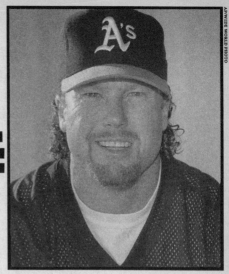

I t was the last day of the 1987 season. Oakland A's first baseman Mark McGwire jumped on a plane and flew from Chicago, where he was supposed to be playing the White Sox at Comiskey Park, to Orange County, California. He got to the hospital delivery room in time for the birth of his son, Matthew.

Mark had hit 49 homers for the Oakland Athletics that year. By skipping the last game, he missed a shot at 50 — a magic number for home-run hitters.

"Everyone said the wind was blowing out that day at Comiskey Park and I would have gotten it," Mark says. "But I said to myself, 'I will never have another firstborn, but I will have another chance to hit 50.'"

It took awhile — nine years, to be exact. But Mark was right. In 1996, he finally hit that magic number. Along the way, Mark struggled with one injury after another. In 1995, he nearly retired. But he didn't give up.

Finally, in 1996, Mark had an awesome season.

Despite missing 32 games, due to injuries, he whacked baseballs with amazing force. The shots rang out in the Oakland Coliseum, where the A's play their home games.

On September 14, Mark bashed his 50th home run, off Chad Ogea [oh-jay] of the Cleveland Indians. He became only the 13th player in history to hit 50 in one season. Afterward, he gave the ball to Matthew.

"Everything I do in life and baseball is for him," Mark says.

◆

Mark was born on October 1, 1963, in Pomona, California. He is the third of five brothers.

Mark's mom, Ginger, was a swimmer in college. His dad, John, had a crippling disease called polio as a child. He spent months in bed, and now wears a leg brace. (In the 1940's and 1950's, millions of kids suffered from polio. Today, due to a vaccine, there are few cases of the disease.)

John McGwire wouldn't let polio ruin his life. He

BLAST FROM THE PAST

Babe Ruth had the most powerful swing the game has ever seen. Babe's home runs earned him the nickname "The Sultan of Swat." He hit a record 60 homers in 1927, and finished his career in 1935 with a record 714 homers (both records have been broken). Babe also hit home runs more often than any other player. He averaged a home run every 11.8 at-bats. Mark McGwire has averaged a home run every 12.4 at-bats — second only to Babe.

became a successful dentist, enjoyed boxing, playing golf, and long-distance cycling. "If you look at what he's gone through in his life and the injuries I've had," Mark says, "well, mine don't equal out to what has happened to him."

When the five McGwire brothers grew up, they grew *up!* The smallest, J.J., is 6' 2". Mark is 6' 5" and weighs 250 pounds. One of Mark's "little" brothers, Dan, is a 6' 8" former quarterback for the Miami Dolphins.

Dr. and Mrs. McGwire made sure their sons worked hard in school and in sports. Mrs. McGwire certainly didn't have to coax her kids to the dinner table. They had *big* appetites. "Mom would have to double or triple every recipe," Mark says.

◆

Before he played baseball, Mark played golf. His father taught him to swing a club when he was 5 years old.

The family moved to Claremont, California, when Mark was 7. He made a good impression right away: In his first Little League at-bat, Mark homered!

Mark became the Babe Ruth of the Claremont Little League. In the 1974 season, he hit a record 13 homers. That record stood for 20 years. He was also an ace pitcher with an overpowering fastball.

Mark hit golf balls a long way, too. As a sophomore at Damien High School, in Claremont, he quit baseball to concentrate on golf. He played on the high school team.

"The thing I liked about golf was that you were the only one there to blame when something went wrong," Mark says. "I missed baseball, though, so I went back to it."

Mark returned to the baseball team his junior year.

Professional baseball scouts loved Mark's arm. In 1981, after his senior year, the Montreal Expos picked him in the eighth round of the draft. The Expos told Mark they wanted him to pitch.

Even so, they didn't offer him enough money to make it worth his while to skip college. Iinstead, Mark took his blazing fastball to the University of Southern California. As a freshman in 1982, Mark won 4 and lost 4. Still, he had a very good 3.04 earned run average.

That summer, he went to Alaska, to play in a summer league. He pitched and played first base. By tightening up his swing — making it shorter — he won the batting title! (That means he had the highest batting average.)

When Mark returned to USC, he started bashing home runs. Soon he wasn't a pitcher anymore. Instead, he concentrated on hitting and playing first base. He set a USC record with 19 homers in 53 games, in 1983, and broke it with 32 in 67 games, in 1984.

The Oakland A's grabbed Mark in the first round of

COOL FACTS In 1991, Mark caddied for pro golfer Billy Andrade at a tournament in Australia. "The Australian caddies were blown away," Mark says. "They couldn't get over how big I was or that I was carrying Billy's bag with one hand instead of slung over my shoulder." With Mark's help, Billy finished fourth. Then, in 1993, Mark and Billy played together in the AT&T Pebble Beach Pro-Am. They finished second!

OTHER PEOPLE SAY . . .

"I honestly believe we're watching the best home-run hitter in the game. To miss one of his at-bats is a real mistake." —A's third baseman Scott Brosius

the 1984 draft. Before turning pro, Mark helped the U.S. baseball team win a gold medal at the 1984 Los Angeles Olympics. (Baseball was not an official medal sport at the 1984 Games. It was played as a "demonstration" sport.)

Mark hit 47 homers in two minor league seasons. He was invited to spring training with the A's in 1987, in spite of manager Tony LaRussa's doubts about his making the team. Mark's hitting changed Tony's mind fast!

"Mark had to play his way onto the team, and he did," Tony said. "We *had* to find a position for him."

Mark's rookie season was amazing! He hit 49 homers, blowing away the old record for homers by a rookie. The old record of 37 was set by Al Rosen of the Cleveland Indians in 1950.

"The only thing Mark lacks is speed," said Jose Canseco, who was a teammate that year and is a fellow power hitter. "But power hitters don't need speed. They just need to jog around the bases." Mark and Jose were known as the Bash Brothers. After a home run, they celebrated by bashing their mighty forearms together.

There was a whole lot of bashing going on. Mark hit 32 homers in 1988, 33 in 1989, and 39 in 1990. The A's went to the World Series all three seasons. In 1989, they won!

In 1991, Mark went into an awful slump. He hit only 22 homers, and his batting average was a pitiful .201.

He took a lot of heat for it. From an elementary school near Mark's house, the kids would yell at him, "McGwire, you stink!"

Later that year, Mark was in the audience at a comedy club. Comedian Mark Pitta picked up a menu. "Look at this," the comedian told the audience. "A Mark McGwire burger. For five-ninety-five. Hmmm. Shouldn't the price be two-oh-one [.201]?"

Instead of being angry, Mark couldn't stop laughing. "Laughter is a great healer," he told Steve Wulf of *Sports Illustrated*. "After that night, I knew I would be all right."

◆

Mark changed his batting stance. He pumped iron. The changes worked. He bopped 42 homers in 1992, and improved his batting average to .268. But the next season, his body began to fall apart. Mark's feet are too narrow for his big body. Muscles on the bottom of his feet began to tear. Mark had foot surgery that limited him to 74 games total for 1993 and 1994. He had more foot pain in 1995.

OTHER PEOPLE SAY . . .

"Mark has not let frustration beat him. He has had some really tough injuries and came back better each time. When you do not play, you can get soft and your skills can erode. But Mark has gotten better, quicker, and stronger." — former A's manager Tony LaRussa

COOL FACTS If he hadn't become a ballplayer, Mark says he would have become a cop. Early in his career with the A's, he rode along with policemen and highway patrolmen in Northern California. He loved watching them bust drug dealers.

When he injured his right heel badly in March 1996, Mark thought about quitting. "My dad and my family told me that if I'd retired, it'd be the biggest mistake of my life," Mark says.

Mark missed 18 games at the start of the season. When he came back, wearing heel supports in both shoes, he started swinging for the fences again. Back pain kept him out of the lineup at times, but in 130 games, he led the majors with 52 homers.

Mark didn't just hit them *out* of the park. He hit them *way out*. Six of his homers traveled more than 450 feet. He hit one 488 feet, which was the longest homer measured in the majors in at least five years.

If Mark had played a full schedule of 162 games, he probably would have broken the major league record for one season of 61 homers. The record was set by Roger Maris of the New York Yankees in 1961.

"I don't sit here thinking about [the home-run record] because I know how difficult it is," Mark says. "I mean, hitting a home run is probably the most difficult thing in sports."

Mark makes it look easy.

48

PERSONAL STATS

Name: Mark David McGwire

Nickname: Big Mac

Height: 6' 5"   **Weight:** 250 lbs.

Bats: Right   **Throws:** Right

Birth Date: October 1, 1963

Birthplace: Pomona, California

Current Home: Alamo, California

Family: Matthew (son, born October 4, 1987).
Mark is divorced from Matthew's mom, Kathy.

MAJOR LEAGUE STATS
OAKLAND A'S

YEAR	AVG.	G	AB	R	H	HR	RBI	SO	BB	SB
1986	.189	18	53	10	10	3	9	18	4	0
1987	.289	151	557	97	161	49	118	131	71	1
1988	.260	155	550	87	143	32	99	117	76	0
1989	.231	143	490	74	113	33	95	94	83	1
1990	.235	156	523	87	123	39	108	116	110	2
1991	.201	154	483	62	97	22	75	116	93	2
1992	.268	139	467	87	125	42	104	105	90	0
1993	.333	27	84	16	28	9	24	19	21	0
1994	.252	47	135	26	34	9	25	40	37	0
1995	.274	104	317	75	87	39	90	77	88	1
1996	.312	130	423	104	132	52	113	112	116	0
TOTAL	.258	1,224	4,082	725	1,053	329	860	945	789	7

ALBERT BELLE

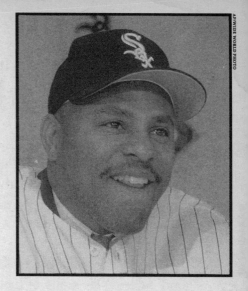

I t often happens late at night, long after a game has ended. Whether his team has won or lost, Albert Belle decides he has more work to do.

One by one, his teammates leave the clubhouse. But Albert isn't ready to go home. Instead, he picks up his bat and trudges off to a batting cage under the stands. There he cranks up the pitching machine.

Albert may have hit a home run that night. He may have had three hits in four at-bats. But he has found some tiny flaw in his swing, and he wants to fix it.

Crack! Crack! Crack! Albert rips ball after ball into the netting of the batting cage. He keeps hitting until he is satisfied, or until the pitching machine runs out of balls. "Albert gets absolutely the most out of every little bit of ability he has," says his twin brother, Terry.

That's why Albert was able to hit more homers (234) and to drive in more runs (711) from 1991 to 1996 than any other major league player. In 1996, Albert whacked

48 homers for the Cleveland Indians. In 1995, he hit 50!

After the 1996 season, Albert left the Indians. He had played for them since 1989. Albert signed a five-year, $55-million contract with the Chicago White Sox. The contract makes him the highest paid player in baseball.

While there's no doubt that Albert is talented, he is also known for being troubled. "Albert Belle is a man with many sides," said Skip Bertman, who coached him at Louisiana State University. "And you never know which angle is tilted your way."

Albert's teammates in Cleveland preferred to see the good angles. "He's one of the most popular guys on this team," said Indian catcher Sandy Alomar, Junior. "There's nobody in here who wants to produce more than he does. Nobody wants to win more. He's just very intense."

◆

Albert and Terry were born four minutes apart on August 25, 1966, in Shreveport, Louisiana. They are fraternal (non-identical) twins.

Their mother, Carrie, was a math teacher, and their father, Albert, Senior, was a high school football coach. Young Albert's middle name was Jojuan [juh-WAHN]. His parents nicknamed him Joey.

The Belles lived in a nice neighborhood. Joey and Terry were popular with the other kids. Joey was smart, and he was very good at sports, especially baseball.

Joey became an Eagle Scout, and then an all-state outfielder for Shreveport's Huntington High School. He graduated sixth in his class. Terry also was a star outfielder for the baseball team. He graduated fifth in his class.

"I brought Joey up to excel in everything," Mrs. Belle has said. "He wants to be perfect."

Joey and Terry both accepted baseball scholarships to Louisiana State University (LSU). The brothers were roommates. As a sophomore in 1986, Joey set an LSU record with 21 homers in 68 games.

As pro scouts started paying more attention to Albert, he became uncomfortable. "There was all this pressure," Pete Bush, an LSU teammate, told Jennifer Frey of *The Washington Post* newspaper. "You could see it get to him."

Joey hit 21 homers again as a junior in 1987. He was expected to be a first-round draft pick. Then, during a Southeastern Conference tournament game in Athens, Georgia, a Mississippi State University fan started yelling racist remarks at Joey. The fan was sitting beyond the outfield fence. When the man yelled "Nigger!" once too often, Joey confronted him. Joey's teammates pulled him back.

Later in that game, Joey smashed a long, looping line drive. He thought it was going over the centerfield fence, so he went into an easy home-run trot. Instead, the

OTHER PEOPLE SAY . . .

"As [my brother] has gotten older and gotten to know the pitchers, he has come to realize that he can't get a hit every at-bat. Even if he's a superstar, he's still going to fail 70 percent of the time — and still be considered a success. He didn't realize that at first." — Terry Belle, Albert's twin ball dropped in, and Joey was held to a single because he hadn't run harder. Because he failed to run all-out, Joey was pulled from the game. Coach Bertman asked Joey to apologize to his teammates. When Joey refused, he was suspended. He never played another game for LSU.

Most teams were afraid to draft Joey after that. Not the Cleveland Indians. They took a chance on him in the second round of the 1987 amateur draft.

◆

Joey went to play in the minor leagues. Minor league pitchers had plenty of trouble getting him out! As a result, it took him only two years to reach the majors. In 1989, he was playing for the Canton-Akron, Ohio, team in the Double-A Eastern League. After 89 games, he was leading the league with 20 homers and 69 runs batted in (RBIs). He was promoted to Cleveland on July 15.

BLAST FROM THE PAST

Like Albert Belle, Richie Allen had a career of ups and downs. Richie hit 20 or more homers 10 times in his 14-year career. But when Richie played third base and first base for the Philadelphia Phillies, from 1963 to 1969, fans booed him a lot. The Phillies were a bad team and the fans blamed Richie. He could never do enough to please them. Richie responded by writing "BOO!" in the dirt with his spikes. Later in his career, Richie told people to call him Dick. With the Chicago White Sox in 1972, Dick Allen hit 37 homers and was named the American League MVP.

Through the rest of 1989, Joey batted only .225 with 7 homers in 62 games for the Indians. He often got angry at himself. Joey snapped so many bats in half over his knee in frustration that other players started calling him "Snapper."

When he struggled early in the 1990 season, Joey was sent back to the minors. After 24 games at Triple-A Colorado Springs, Joey made a shocking announcement. He said he had a drinking problem, and he asked for a leave of absence to get treatment for alcoholism.

Joey spent two months in the Cleveland Clinic. When he got out, he decided he wanted to start over. He even wanted to change his name. He decided he wanted to be called by his real name: Albert.

"He had a problem, and he came to terms with it," said Indian general manager John Hart. "That's in the past. Albert Belle is the most popular player in Cleveland. He does what we pay him to do."

Albert returned to Cleveland with a bang. In 1991, he hit 28 homers and drove in 95 runs. Every year, his performance has improved. But every year, he also did something that made people think he was a bad person.

In 1991, Albert was suspended for throwing a ball at a fan who was yelling at him. In 1992 and 1993, he was suspended for charging the mound. (Albert ran toward the pitcher because he felt the pitcher was throwing at him.) In 1994, he was suspended because there was cork inside his bat. A bat that has been hollowed out and filled with cork is lighter and easier to swing. It is also against the rules. Albert denied having put the cork inside his bat.

Even when things were going well, Albert has had

problems. In 1995, Albert had a great year. He hit .317 with 50 homers, the most homers in the major leagues, and 126 RBIs. He led the Indians into the World Series. They had not been to the Series since 1954.

Albert refused to talk to reporters during the Series. At one point, he cursed at television reporter Hannah Storm. He was fined $50,000. Cleveland lost the Series to the powerful Atlanta Braves, four games to two.

During spring training in 1996, he threw a ball at a *Sports Illustrated* magazine photographer. He was ordered to undergo counseling to deal with his anger or face suspension.

All this didn't keep Albert from batting .311 with 48 homers and 148 RBIs in 158 games in 1996. Then he signed his big contract with the White Sox.

Because Albert doesn't often talk to reporters, fans don't know much about him. He likes to work crossword puzzles, and he enjoys golf, bowling, Ping-Pong, and chess.

At first, Albert was a lousy Ping-Pong player. But he kept playing until he became the Indians' clubhouse champ!

"He's not afraid of failure," former teammate Wayne Kirby once said. "In fact, it's the opposite. He knows failure comes around and turns into success if you work at it. And he works as hard as anyone I've seen."

Albert doesn't work only at sports. He is just a few credits shy of earning his accounting degree from Cleveland State University. He donates his time and money to a wide variety of charities. "He's the greatest thing since folded napkins," Mimi Shenk of the United

Way charity told *USA Today* newspaper in 1994. "The kids love him. I can't say enough good things about him. He's shy. He loves children. He gets hit, if you will, in the media, because he's not a Michael Jordan. That doesn't make him unkind. It makes him more like the rest of us."

In 1993, Cleveland pitchers Steve Olin and Tim Crews died in a boating accident at spring training. It was Albert who led the team's prayers in the clubhouse.

On road trips, Albert has been known to perform a rap song called "Potbelly Nellie." It pokes good-natured fun at Indian first-base coach Dave Nelson. But Coach Nelson has also been on the receiving end of Albert's sharp tongue.

"Albert has snapped at me," Coach Nelson told *Sports Illustrated* in 1996. "You never know which Albert is going to show up. Sometimes he's laughing with everybody, and sometimes he wants to be off by himself, doing the crossword puzzle.

"It's hard to understand what makes him tick."

Albert doesn't seem to care if people understand him or not. He would rather pound baseballs over the fence.

That he does very, very well.

COOL FACTS Albert writes the result of every one of his at-bats on three-by-five-inch index cards. He keeps the cards in a file in his locker. That way Albert can prepare for his *next* at-bat against a certain pitcher by going over what he did in *earlier* at-bats against that pitcher.

PERSONAL STATS

Name: Albert Jojuan Belle
Height: 6' 2"   **Weight:** 210 lbs.
Bats: Right   **Throws:** Right
Birth Date: August 25, 1966
Birthplace: Shreveport, Louisiana
Current Home: Euclid, Ohio
Family: Carrie (mother), Albert, Senior (father),
Terry (brother)

MAJOR LEAGUE STATS
CLEVELAND INDIANS

YEAR	AVG.	G	AB	R	H	HR	RBI	SO	BB	SB
1989	.225	62	218	22	49	7	37	55	12	2
1990	.174	9	23	1	4	1	3	6	1	0
1991	.282	123	461	60	130	28	95	99	25	3
1992	.260	153	585	81	152	34	112	128	52	8
1993	.290	159	594	93	172	38	129	96	76	23
1994	.357	106	412	90	147	36	101	71	58	9
1995	.317	143	546	121	173	50	126	80	73	5
1996	.311	158	602	124	187	48	148	87	99	11
TOTAL	.295	913	3,441	592	1,014	242	751	622	396	61

CECIL FIELDER

In June 1996, Cecil Fielder of the Detroit Tigers was interviewed by young reporters for *Sports Illustrated For Kids* magazine. Cecil *[SESS-uhl]* was bummed out. He dreamed of playing in a World Series. But as long as he was stuck with the terrible Tigers, his dream would never come true.

"I'm a competitive person," Cecil told the kids. "I *hate* losing."

A few weeks later, Cecil was traded from the worst team in baseball to one of the best: the New York Yankees! "I have a shot at playing in the World Series. Is this really happening?" he asked.

It was happening, all right. In October, Cecil would finally have a starring role on baseball's biggest stage.

◆

Cecil Fielder is a powerful first baseman. He is 6' 3" tall, and he weighs *at least* 260 pounds. His nickname is Big Daddy.

Like the rest of us, Big Daddy was once a baby. Cecil was born in Los Angeles, California, on September 21, 1963. His mother, Tina, thought he might grow up to be a big man. "You should see his four uncles," Mrs. Fielder told *Sports Illustrated* in 1991. "I'm afraid we're a big family." Each uncle weighs more than 200 pounds.

Cecil was a tall, heavy kid. But he was very athletic. He starred on the football team as a linebacker. But basketball was his favorite sport. Cecil was a 6' 3" point guard for Nogales High School, in La Puente, California. He could even dunk!

"I didn't even *like* baseball," Cecil says. "I played one year when I was seven, and I thought it was very boring. I didn't get back into it until my junior year of high school. Before that, I chased girls during baseball season."

◆

When Cecil got back into baseball, he found he could do it well. Maybe that's why he was named "Most Athletic" in his high school class! Cecil quickly became a

COOL FACTS In 1995, Cecil and his family moved into the largest private home in Brevard County, Florida. It has 50 rooms! The mansion includes three fireplaces, a movie theater, a two-story walk-in closet, an indoor waterfall, a sauna, a steam room, a tennis court, a swimming pool, and a six-car garage. Cecil and his wife, Stacey, call it home. Their children, Prince and Ceclyn, call it "Disney World."

OTHER PEOPLE SAY . . .
"Cecil is fun to have around. He's the kind of guy you root for even when he's not on your team."
— Yankee outfielder Paul O'Neill

star for the Nogales High baseball team. His long home runs got him noticed. They earned him a scholarship to the University of Nevada-Las Vegas (UNLV).

Cecil lasted one semester at UNLV before he dropped out. Then he tried a junior college, Mount San Antonio, in Walnut, California. He played on its baseball team the spring after he left UNLV, but he left Mount San Antonio, too. He was tired of school.

Baseball scouts had seen enough of Cecil to consider him a major league prospect. The Kansas City Royals picked him in the fourth round of the 1982 draft. That summer, Cecil hit 20 homers in 69 games for a Royals rookie league team in Butte, Montana. The Royals traded him to the Toronto Blue Jays in February 1983.

Cecil moved up a notch each year in the Blue Jay farm system. He was promoted to the majors near the end of the 1985 season. Cecil played for Toronto through 1988, but he didn't play much.

Cecil had two problems in Toronto. First, the Blue Jays had another very good first baseman — Fred McGriff. Second, manager Jimy Williams thought Cecil was too fat.

"The manager made an issue of my weight," Cecil

says. "He had me running with the pitchers. They had me weighing in every other day."

The Blue Jays didn't understand. Cecil may look fat — heck, he may even *be* fat — but that doesn't stop him from hitting homers into the lights. It doesn't stop him from being a better-than-average fielder at first base, either.

◆

To get a chance to play every day, Cecil had to go all the way to Japan. The Blue Jays sold his contract to the Hanshin Tigers and convinced Cecil it would be a good opportunity for him. They were right. In 1989, Cecil became one of the biggest stars in Japanese baseball. He smashed 38 homers.

"I loved it there," Cecil says. "I ate a lot of different foods, such as *sushi* and *sashimi* [raw fish], and *yaki soba* [noodles]. My family went to all the different amusement parks. They took Japanese lessons, and my wife did a little acting. I think that year made me a better person and a better player."

BLAST FROM THE PAST

When Cecil Fielder was a kid, his favorite player was Willie McCovey of the San Francisco Giants. Like Cecil, Willie was a big man. The 6' 4", 215-pound first baseman was nicknamed "Stretch." In his 22-season career, from 1959 to 1980, he hit 521 home runs. Willie led the National League in homers three times. In 1969, when he batted .320 with 45 homers and 126 RBIs, Willie was the N.L. Most Valuable Player.

OTHER PEOPLE SAY . . .

"When we traded for Cecil, the guys couldn't wait for him to get here. He's a presence in the clubhouse, that's for sure!" — Yankee manager Joe Torre

Cecil hoped that his experience in Japan would make the major league teams line up to sign him. They didn't.

"Too many teams were worried about my weight," he says. "Detroit only signed me after two other guys turned them down."

Detroit manager Sparky Anderson thought Cecil would have to be a designated hitter. "He was just a great big man, and I'm saying to myself, 'How in the heck is he going to play first base?'" Sparky says. "But then I noticed how quick he was, and what outstanding hands he has. Then I knew we had a first baseman."

They also had a slugger. Cecil crushed a major league high 51 homers in 1990. He became only the 11th man to hit 50 or more in a season. The following year he hit 44 to lead the majors again.

Everyone wondered whether Cecil's size made him so great. "It really doesn't matter how big you are," he says. "What matters is how fast you get that bat through the strike zone."

Cecil never tries to hit homers. He tries to make good contact, and keep the ball in play. When a game is on the line, he is just as happy to drive in runs with a single as with a homer. With 132 runs batted in (RBIs) in 1990, 133 in

1991, and 124 in 1992, Cecil became the first man since Babe Ruth to lead the majors in that category three years in a row. Through 1996, Cecil had more homers (258) and RBIs (795) than any other player during the 1990s!

That's why the Yankees traded outfielder Ruben Sierra on July 31, 1996, to get Cecil from Detroit. Although the Yankees were in first place, owner George Steinbrenner didn't think they were scoring enough runs.

Cecil got an apartment in Manhattan. Yankee fans were happy to have him on board. Wherever he went, they wanted to slap him on the back or give him a high five.

"Everyone knows I'm a good guy, but you hear things about the Yankees and you don't know what to expect," Cecil says. "You hear it might be stressful. I don't see it. Once I got here and all the boys were vibing and loose, it made it easier to free up my mind."

Cecil hit 13 homers in 53 games for the Yanks. The team finished first in the American League East. The Yankees outgunned the Texas Rangers in the division series, and then beat the Baltimore Orioles in five games for the pennant. In the eight games he played in those two playoff series, Cecil hit three homers and drove in 12 runs.

At last, Cecil was heading for the World Series. The

COOL FACTS Cecil is the only active major leaguer known to have hit a homer more than 500 feet. He did it on September 14, 1991, at Milwaukee's County Stadium. The ball traveled 502 feet. Now *that's* power!

spotlight was on, and he would be in it! *"This* is what it's all about," he said.

The Yankees lost the first two games to the Atlanta Braves, and most people thought the Series was over. Not Big Daddy. "Hey, we can win this thing," he told his team-mates in the clubhouse before Game 3. He was right!

Even though he didn't hit any homers, Cecil's hot bat helped the Yankees sweep the next four games and win the Series! Cecil delivered nine hits in 23 at-bats, for a team-high .391 average. In the Yankees' 1–0 Game 5 win, his fourth-inning double drove in the only run.

When the Yankees clinched the Series, in Game Six, Big Daddy ran onto the field and jumped for joy. "I've made it," Cecil said.

He also earned himself a World Series ring. A *big* one!

PERSONAL STATS

Name: Cecil Grant Fielder
Nickname: Big Daddy
Birth Date: September 21, 1963
Birthplace: Los Angeles, California
Current Home: Suntree, Florida
Height: 6' 3"　　　**Weight:** 260 lbs.
Bats: Right　　　**Throws:** Right
Family: Stacey (wife); Prince (son, born May 9, 1984); Ceclyn (daughter, born February 20, 1992)

MAJOR LEAGUE STATS
TORONTO BLUE JAYS

YEAR	AVG.	G	AB	R	H	HR	RBI	SO	BB	SB
1985	.311	30	74	6	23	4	16	16	6	0
1986	.157	34	83	7	13	4	13	27	6	0
1987	.269	82	175	30	47	14	32	48	20	0
1988	.230	74	174	24	40	9	23	53	14	0

DETROIT TIGERS

YEAR	AVG.	G	AB	R	H	HR	RBI	SO	BB	SB
1990	.277	159	573	104	159	51	132	182	90	0
1991	.261	162	624	102	163	44	133	151	78	0
1992	.244	155	594	80	145	35	124	151	73	0
1993	.267	154	573	80	153	30	117	125	90	0
1994	.259	109	425	67	110	28	90	110	50	0
1995	.243	136	494	70	120	31	82	116	75	0
1996	.248	107	391	55	97	26	80	91	63	2

NEW YORK YANKEES

YEAR	AVG.	G	AB	R	H	HR	RBI	SO	BB	SB
1996	.260	53	200	30	52	13	37	48	24	0
TOTAL	.256	1,255	4,380	655	1,122	289	879	1,118	589	2